BOOK CLUB EDITION

ANIMALS
do the
STRANGEST
THINGS

by
Leonora and Arthur Hornblow

Illustrations by Michael K. Frith

RANDOM HOUSE STEP-UP BOOKS NEW YORK

FOR STEVEN HORNBLOW

7 368

Table of Contents

Never Thirsty (The Camel)   **3**

The King (The Lion)   **6**

Tallest on Earth (The Giraffe)   **8**

The Man-Eater (The Tiger)   **14**

The Happy Ones (The Sea Otter)   **16**

Living Radar (The Little Brown Bat)   **18**

Playing Dead (The Opossum)   **22**

The Biggest Ever (The Blue Whale)   **24**

The Mild Monster (The Gorilla)   **26**

In the Deep Freeze (The Polar Bear)   **32**

Small But Mighty (The Skunk)   **38**

Pack Hunters (The Wolf)   **40**

The Riddle (The Platypus)   **42**

Upside Down (The Sloth)   **48**

Strange Journey (The Lemming)   **49**

Big Blubber (The Elephant Seal)   **50**

Never Trust a Bear (The Black Bear)   **52**

The Gentle Giant (The Elephant)   **56**

Flying Fur (The Flying Squirrel)   **62**

2

Never Thirsty

There are great deserts of sand in Arabia and Africa. They are hot and dry. Water holes are far apart. Men could not get far on the desert without help. But they have the help of the camel.

The camel can carry a man and a heavy load. And the camel does not mind living in the desert. This is because he can do many strange things that other animals cannot do.

Sometimes, out in the desert, the winds blow. Then the sand gets into everything. It gets into people's eyes. It gets into their ears and noses. But the sand does not get into the camel's eyes. He has long eyelashes to keep it out. It does not get into his ears. He has hair in his ears to keep it out. And he can just close up his nose. The camel's mouth is not soft like most animals'. He can eat spiny desert plants. And he does.

The camel has big flat feet. They do not sink into the soft sand.

He can walk thirty miles in a day. He can do this without eating or drinking. He can go without food or water for many days.

The camel needs food and water. But he does not need them as often as other animals do. When he has food he eats a lot. He stores it in the hump on his back. When there is water he drinks a lot. He stores it in other parts of his body. Then he uses the food and water as he needs them.

The camel is not friendly. He does not care about man. But for the people of the desert he is a very important animal.

The King

The lion is called the "King of the Beasts." He is big and strong. Around his neck there is a great mane of hair. He is the most noble-looking animal of all.

But the lion is not the bravest animal. He will never go into a camp where there is a fire. And he runs from anything that flaps in the wind.

And the noble lion lets his wife
do most of the work.

He does help her in one way. He
roars. His roar scares other animals.
They run away from the lion. They
run right toward the lioness. The
lion waits while she does the killing.
Then he joins her for dinner.

Tallest on Earth

Some animals are pretty. Others are ugly. But the giraffe is just fantastic!

Giraffes have very long thin legs. They have very, very long necks. Giraffes are the tallest living animals in the world.

Thanks to his long
neck and his long legs,
the giraffe can see everything
around him. He can keep a sharp
lookout for his enemies. His
enemies are lions and leopards.

It is strange that
the giraffe's enemies
often do not see him.
A giraffe's skin
color helps him to
hide. He feeds in the
tall trees and grass.
If he stands very
still he seems almost
like a tree himself.

The giraffe fights only if he must. If an enemy comes too near the giraffe runs away. He is clumsy, but he is very fast. If he has to fight he uses his long legs and sharp feet. He kicks his enemy. Sometimes he hits his enemy with his strong neck.

The giraffe's long neck and legs are a very great help to him. But they are a problem to him, too. Every time he takes a drink of water he is in trouble. Every time he takes a drink he is afraid.

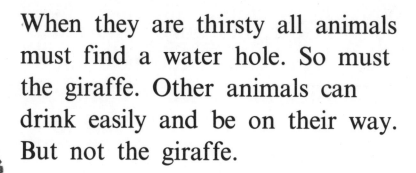

When they are thirsty all animals must find a water hole. So must the giraffe. Other animals can drink easily and be on their way. But not the giraffe.

For there is a very strange thing about the giraffe. He cannot kneel down to reach the water. And it is hard for him to get his legs apart. He has to do it slowly, in stiff, clumsy jerks. This is the only way he can get to the water to drink it.

While he is doing this he cannot run away. He cannot fight. A lion or leopard could kill him easily. So, when he has to drink, he is very careful. He always makes sure that no other animals are near.

Cows moo. Lions roar. But most giraffes cannot make a sound. You can be very near a lot of giraffes and never know they are there. But they will know that you are there. They might even come over to see you. Giraffes are like many people. They always want to know what is going on.

The Man-Eater

There are many wild animals that kill men. They kill men because they are afraid of them. They do not kill them for food. They do not like the way people taste.

But in the jungle it is not always easy to find animals to kill. Then a tiger may kill a man for food.

Not all tigers are man-eaters. Often man-eaters are old tigers. Or they may be tigers that have been sick or hurt.

They find they are not as strong as they once were. They cannot kill the animals they usually eat. Then they go after people. People are much easier for a tiger to kill than any other animal.

A tiger who eats a man learns to like the taste. From then on he is a man-eater!

The Happy Ones

The water where the sea otters live is cold. There are big waves. But the sea otters don't mind. They love to play in the waves. They chase each other. They race. And they dive for shellfish.

When an otter comes up, he doesn't just bring shellfish. He brings a flat rock, too. He lies on his back in the water. He puts the rock on his chest. He bangs the shellfish on the rock. He bangs until the shellfish breaks open. Then he can eat the soft meat inside.

Sea otters live a wonderful, happy life in the sea. They even sleep in the sea. They just close their eyes and go to sleep on their backs.

Living Radar

Birds can fly. So can bats. But bats are not birds. They are mammals. They are the only mammals that can fly.

Birds' wings are made of feathers. Bats' wings are made of skin. There is skin between their long fingers. When they open their arms the skin stretches out. Their arms become wings.

The little brown bat eats insects.
Every year bats eat billions of
insects. Because of this they are
good friends to man.

Bats sleep in dark caves or lonely
barns. They sleep all day. And
they sleep in a strange way. They
hang upside down.

When night comes they wake up.
Then they go out looking for
insects. They fly very fast. They
catch the insects as they fly.

Sometimes women are afraid of
bats. They are afraid that bats will
fly into their hair. But this almost
never happens. The reason is quite
wonderful.

As the bat flies he makes a very
high squeak. The sound goes ahead
of him. It hits anything in his way.
It bounces right back. The bat hears
it bounce back. In this way he knows
there is something there. There may
be thousands of flying bats in a
great black cave. But one bat never
bumps into another.

There is a saying, "Blind as a bat."
But bats are not blind. They can see
with their eyes and they can see
with their ears.

Playing Dead

The opossum has a really strange way of keeping himself safe. He makes believe he is dead.

Many animals hunt other animals for food. Most of them like to catch their food alive. The opossum knows this. When an enemy comes too near the opossum doesn't move. His enemy thinks he is dead. The opossum stays still until his enemy goes away.

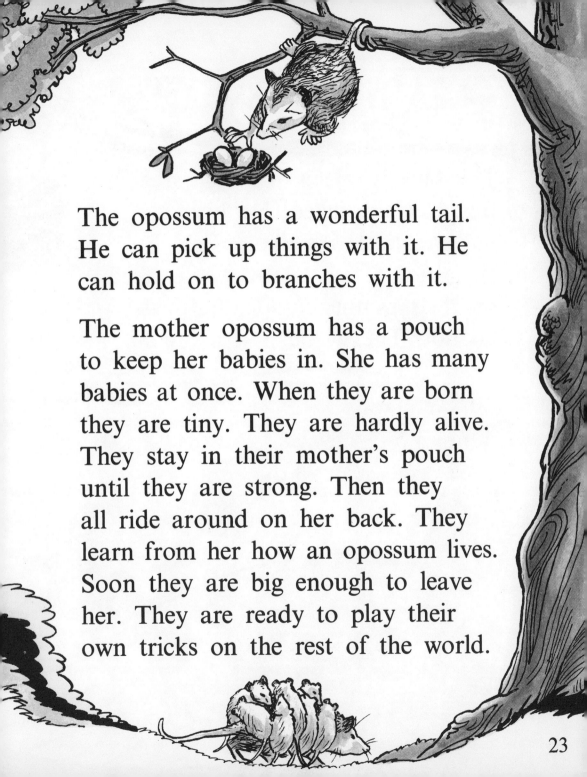

The opossum has a wonderful tail.
He can pick up things with it. He
can hold on to branches with it.

The mother opossum has a pouch
to keep her babies in. She has many
babies at once. When they are born
they are tiny. They are hardly alive.
They stay in their mother's pouch
until they are strong. Then they
all ride around on her back. They
learn from her how an opossum lives.
Soon they are big enough to leave
her. They are ready to play their
own tricks on the rest of the world.

The Biggest Ever

The blue whale is the biggest animal that has ever lived. He lives in the sea and he looks like a fish. But he is not a fish. Baby whales feed on their mother's milk. Baby fish do not. The whale is a mammal.

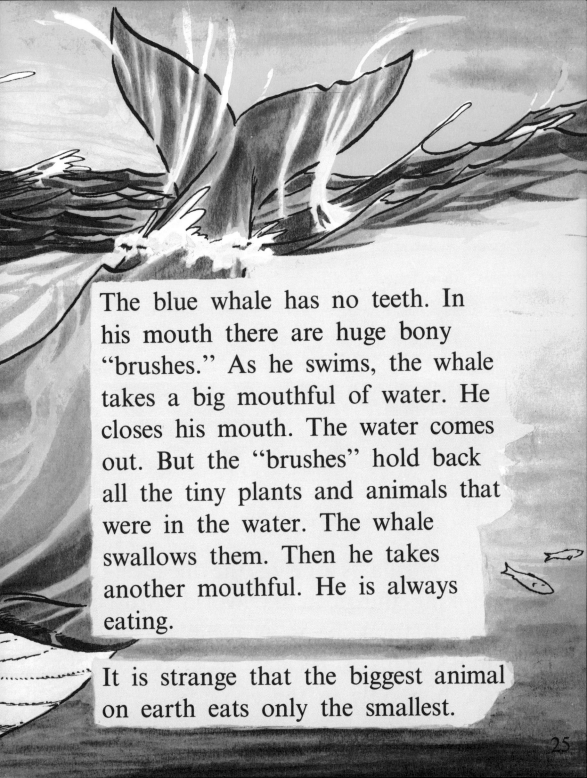

The blue whale has no teeth. In his mouth there are huge bony "brushes." As he swims, the whale takes a big mouthful of water. He closes his mouth. The water comes out. But the "brushes" hold back all the tiny plants and animals that were in the water. The whale swallows them. Then he takes another mouthful. He is always eating.

It is strange that the biggest animal on earth eats only the smallest.

The Mild Monster

The gorilla is one of the meanest-looking things in the world. Most people think he is as mean as he looks. This is because most people see him only in the zoo.

In a zoo the gorilla is very unhappy. He may try to kill anything that comes too close to him. He often tries to break out of his cage. He is very, very strong. This is why a gorilla's cage always has extra-strong bars.

But in his home the gorilla is very different. His home is in the mountains and jungles of Africa.

27

Here he is quiet and gentle. He
has a fine life with his wife and
children. They move slowly along,
looking for food. They eat leaves
and fruit. They do not hurt
anything that does not try to
hurt them.

Every night the gorillas have a
new sleeping place. They make a
kind of nest in the low branches
of a tree. The mother and children
sleep there. The father stays on the
ground. He sleeps at the foot of the
tree. From there he can keep his
wife and children safe.

The gorilla's life is not always
quiet. Sometimes the father
gorilla does a very strange thing.
In a way it is a kind of dance.
First he makes a soft hooting noise.
Then he picks a leaf and holds it
in his lips. He stands up high on
his back legs. He hoots faster. He
throws leaves in the air. He hits
his great chest so hard the noise
can be heard far away. He kicks
one leg in the air. He runs
sideways. He rips leaves and
branches off trees. Then, to end
it all, he hits the ground with
his mighty hand.

No one knows why the father gorilla does this. When he does, his wife and children stay well away. But he does not do it very often. Most of the time the gorilla lives a gentle life. In his jungle home, happy and free, he is a very mild monster.

In the Deep Freeze

Up near the North Pole it is very cold. The cold winds blow and blow. They never stop. All year long there is snow and ice everywhere.

There are bears that live near the North Pole. They are called polar bears.

A strange thing about the polar
bear is that he loves the cold.
Other bears live in cold places.
But they don't like it. When winter
comes they hurry to warm caves.
They sleep there until the spring.
Sometimes they don't even wake up
to eat.

Not the polar bear. They are always
out in the cold. Except when their
babies are born.

Then the mother polar bear gets into a big snow drift. The snow is like a blanket over her. It keeps out the wind and cold. The little polar bear is born under the snow in the middle of winter.

The mother and baby stay in the snow drift until spring. Then they come out into the cold world.

Polar bears swim so well they can catch fish right in the water. But they will eat anything they can find. They will even eat sea weed. On many days dinner will be a seal or a walrus. The polar bear can catch a seal by creeping across the ice. He moves as softly as a cat. Or he may swim up on the seal under the water. He swims very fast and without a sound.

Even when it is very cold and wet
the polar bear stays warm and dry.
There are many things which help
him to live in the ice and snow.

There are layers of fat under his
skin. And there are spaces of air
in his thick white fur. The fat and
the air spaces hold in the heat of
his body. There is also oil in his
fur. This keeps it from getting wet.
There is even fur on the bottom of
his feet. This lets him walk on the
ice and not slip.

When we see polar bears in the zoo in the summer we may worry about them. We know how much they love the cold. But when they are taken away from the north they change. Their fur gets thinner. The oil in it dries up. The fat under their skin goes away.

But they still stay white and beautiful. They still walk lightly on their feet. They like to play in the pools in their cages. When we see them we may be sure that they are the happiest and coolest bears in town.

Small But Mighty

The skunk is a small animal. He is not strong. He cannot run very fast. It would seem that most other animals could kill him easily. But few animals will try it.

The skunk has a very strong weapon. In his body there are two little sacs. From these he can spray a most terrible smell.

Even the skunk doesn't like the smell! He uses it only if he must.

First he stands up on his front
feet. Then he lifts his tail as
high as he can. He is trying to
keep it away from the spray. He
still waits. He hopes the other
animal will leave.

But sometimes the other animal
doesn't leave. Then the skunk
sprays his smell.

Dogs are the only animals that
never seem to learn. They get
sprayed again and again. But most
other animals need to be sprayed
only once. Then they know enough
to leave the little skunk alone!

Pack Hunters

Who is afraid of the big, bad wolf?
A moose is. A moose is much bigger
than a wolf. He has great horns to
help him fight. But he is not safe
from the wolf.

A wolf does not try to fight a moose
all by himself. He joins up with
about sixteen other wolves. They are
called a "pack." They run ahead of
the moose. They wait for him.

When the moose comes the wolves rush out. They make a circle around him. The moose fights back. But they jump on him from all sides.

Then suddenly they stop. They seem to go away. The moose is tired and hurt. He is glad they have gone. He walks on. But the wolves are waiting for him. They attack. They do this again and again. At last the moose is too weak to fight them any more. Then the wolves pull him down.

The wolf pack works like a team. Each wolf knows just what to do. Many big animals are afraid of them. They are the terror of the north country.

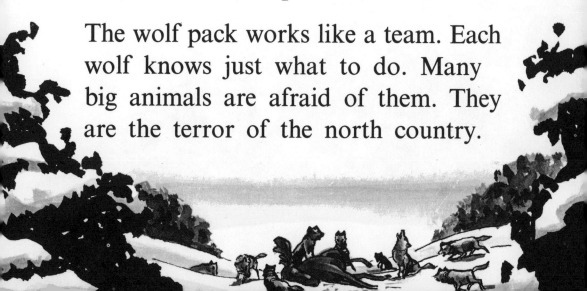

The Riddle

When the duck-billed platypus was first found, nobody could believe it was real.

The platypus has a bill like a bird's and it lays eggs. But it is not a bird.

The platypus has sharp spurs on his legs. There is poison in these spurs. It can kill a small animal. It can hurt a person very badly. Many snakes have poison. But the platypus is not a snake.

The platypus has webbed feet. These make him a fine swimmer. He can swim as well as a fish. But he is not a fish.

The platypus seems to be a bit of everything. But he has hair. And the babies feed on their mother's milk. In these ways he is like all mammals. And so the platypus is a mammal too.

You may never see a platypus. It is very hard to keep them alive in zoos. And they are very shy. They come out only when it is dark.

The platypus spends most of his
life under water. He finds all of
his food under water. To find it
he uses his bill as a shovel. He
digs in the mud for worms and bugs.

The platypus always lives near the water. He digs a long tunnel. The tunnel has two doors. One is on land. The other is under water. This way the platypus can come and go without being seen.

Inside the tunnel the mother platypus makes her nest. She makes it out of weeds and grass. She closes the tunnel with walls of mud. Then she lays her eggs.

The platypus is a riddle. Once there were many animals as strange as he is. But the world has changed since then. The animals on it have changed. Today there is no other animal like the platypus. It may be that he is something left over from a long, long time ago.

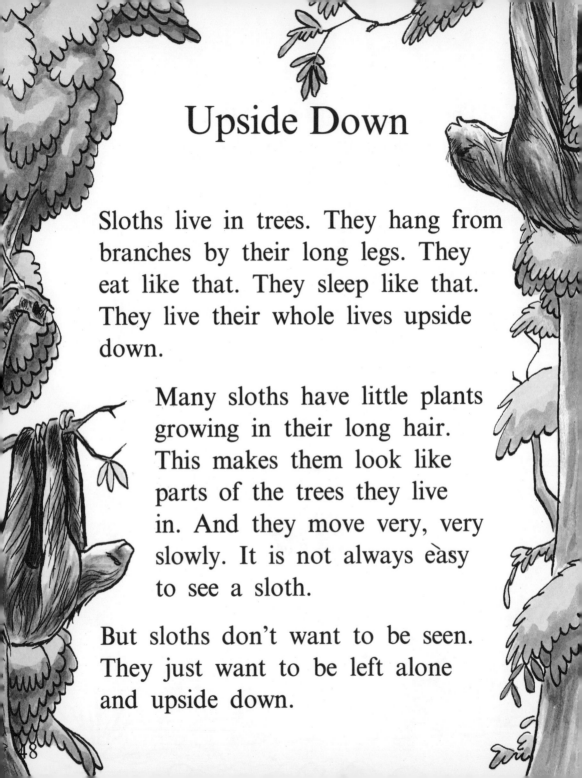

Upside Down

Sloths live in trees. They hang from branches by their long legs. They eat like that. They sleep like that. They live their whole lives upside down.

Many sloths have little plants growing in their long hair. This makes them look like parts of the trees they live in. And they move very, very slowly. It is not always easy to see a sloth.

But sloths don't want to be seen. They just want to be left alone and upside down.

Strange Journey

Lemmings live in the mountains of Norway. Every few years thousands of them suddenly march toward the sea.

No one knows why the lemming makes this strange journey. The sea is far away from the mountains. The lemmings have never seen it. But they go on and on until they reach it. Then they jump in!

They swim out, away from the land. They seem to want to go somewhere. But there is nowhere to go. They cannot swim very well. They soon drown in the cold water.

Big Blubber

The elephant seal gets his name from his nose. His nose looks like a short elephant trunk. He can puff up his nose. He does this when he is frightened or angry.

Elephant seals are so fat, they can hardly move. Their little front flippers are no help to them. So when an elephant seal wants to move on land, he does it in a very strange way.

He sends a ripple over his great, fat body. It goes from his head to his tail. It pushes him a little way. He does it again. It takes a long time for him to get anywhere.

Elephant seals are better off in the water. They swim with their small back flippers. They do not use their front flippers at all.

The elephant seal's only real enemy is in the sea. It is a kind of whale called the killer whale. But on land he is not afraid of anything. So if you ever see one, you can say hello and pat him. He won't mind. But don't ask him to take a walk with you. He would rather sit.

Never Trust a Bear

Grizzly bears and
Alaskan brown bears
are very, very big.
They look dangerous.
They are bears that
no one would trust.

But the American black bears are not
so big. They look clumsy and sweet.
They look like fun to play with. But
playing with a bear would be a bad
mistake.

In a way bears are more dangerous than tigers. Tigers look mean. They sound mean. We can tell that we should stay away from them.

Not bears. Their faces never change. They always look friendly and funny. But they are not. They cannot be trusted at all. They can kill with one blow. They can bite off an arm with their sharp teeth. And they might.

A bear cub grows up fighting for
his food. Most animal mothers
bring food to their babies. Not the
mother bear. She takes her babies
to the food. If it is alive the cub
must kill it himself. He learns to
hit it so it cannot move away.
A bear can knock a swimming fish
out of the water. Bears are very
fast and very strong.

54

So it is never safe to hand food to a bear. He may hit at it. He thinks it might move away.

Kindness doesn't mean anything to a bear. No bear has ever learned to love the people who care for it. And no zoo keeper has ever learned to love a bear.

The Gentle Giant

There are many strange and wonderful things about the elephant. One strange thing about the elephant is his trunk. The elephant's trunk is also his nose. What a nose! Only an elephant has a finger at the end of his nose.

Some elephants have one finger. Some have two. But all elephants can pick up peanuts with their noses without cracking the peanut shells.

And that is not all an elephant
can do with his nose. His nose
is so strong he can pull down a
tree with it.

And only an elephant can fill his
nose with water and give himself
a shower bath.

The elephant's nose
is very strange.
But there are
many other strange
and wonderful things
about the elephant.

The elephant is the biggest four-footed animal in the world. But he can walk as quietly as a mouse. An elephant can walk right by a hunter and not be heard.

All elephants are very smart. Elephants can be taught to carry people on their backs. They will also let people ride on their heads.

Elephants have very big ears. When an elephant is hot, he fans himself with his big ears.

And all elephants can sleep standing up.

People say that elephants never forget. This is so if they have been hurt by someone. An elephant never forgets a man who has been mean to him. That man had better not come too close. The elephant will use his nose as a weapon.

He throws the man down with his nose. He holds him there. He stamps on him with his two front feet. But most elephants will not do this without a good reason.

When one elephant is hurt, the other elephants often try to get him on his feet. They bring him leaves and berries and branches to eat. They take care of him until he is well again.

Elephants are kind to each other.
They are kind to people, too.
People who are nice to the elephant
find the dear, long-nosed, gentle
giant one of man's best friends in
the animal world.

Flying Fur

We have looked at many strange animals in this book. Most of them live far away from us. We see them only in zoos. But one of the strangest animals of all may live right near your home.

He is the little flying squirrel. He does not really fly. He jumps. He spreads his legs. This spreads two folds of skin on the sides of his body. These help him to glide from tree to tree. He steers with his tail.

Flying squirrels are not easy to see. They come out at night. And they move quickly. But they are there.

And so are many other strange
and wonderful things. You just
have to keep your eyes open.
You just have to know where
to look.